La Vera Cucina

(The True Kitchen)

Andiamo a Mangiare!! (Let's Go Eat!!)

Joanne Pecoraro

To order additional copies of this book, contact:
Xlibris
844-714-8691
www.Xlibris.com
Orders@Xlibris.com

ISBN: Softcover   978-1-4415-1918-4
         Hardcover   978-1-4415-1919-1
         EBook   979-8-3694-1652-5

Library of Congress Control Number: 2009902426

Print information available on the last page

Rev. date: 02/12/2024

APPETIZERS

Caponata Siciliana

4 medium eggplants
1 ½ cups olive oil
4 medium onions, sliced
½ cup tomato sauce
4 celery stalks, diced
½ cup capers
12 green olives, pitted and cut
2 tbsp pine nuts
½ cup red wine vinegar
¼ cup sugar
1 tsp salt
½ tsp black pepper

Peel and dice the eggplants. In a large skillet, fry the eggplants in 1 cup of the olive oil, until golden brown. When all of the eggplants are fried, remove them from the skillet and set them aside. Add the remaining oil to the skillet, and lightly brown the onions. Add the tomato sauce and celery, and cook until just tender. If necessary, add a little water. Add the capers, eggplants, olives, and pine nuts to the tomato sauce.

Heat the vinegar in a small saucepan. Dissolve the sugar into the vinegar. Once completely dissolved, pour the vinegar over the eggplants and other vegetable mixture. Add salt and pepper, and simmer for 25 minutes, stirring frequently. Serve cold.

Caponata will keep in an airtight container in the refrigerator for 1 month.

Buon appetito!

Giardiniera
(Pickled Vegetables)

20 carrots, peeled and sliced ½ inch lengthwise

1 bunch of celery, cleaned and cut 1 inch lengthwise

1 medium green pepper and 1 medium red pepper, seeds removed and cut into 2 inch strips

1 medium cauliflower, stems trimmed, cut into florets

12 small pickling onions

¼ cup mustard seed

2 tbsp celery seed

1 small dried red chili pepper

12 small fresh banana peppers

2 ½ qts white vinegar

4 qts water

3 cups sugar

1 cup salt

8 sterilized mason jars

In a medium pot, stir the salt and water together until the salt is dissolved. Add the carrots, celery, cauliflower, green and red peppers, onions, and banana peppers. Cover and refrigerate for 2 days. Afterward, drain and rinse the vegetables TWICE. In a 6-quart Dutch oven, pour the vinegar, mustard seed, celery seed, chili, and sugar, and bring to a boil. Cook for 5 minutes, then add all of the vegetables and cook until they are tender. Remove the red chili.

Keep the mason jars in hot water until they are ready to be filled. Fill the mason jars with the vegetables, using a slotted spoon, and pressing the vegetables down with the spoon as you fill. Pour a little of the vinegar mixture into the jar--just until about half an inch from the rim. Cover the jar with a lid and seal it tightly. Continue the procedure until all the jars are filled.

Store the sealed jars in a cool, dry place. Once opened, store giardiniera in the refrigerator. Giardiniera will last 3 to 4 weeks in the refrigerator.

Buon appetito!

Polpette di patate e tonno
(Potato and Tuna Appetizer)

4 large potatoes, boiled and mashed

4 celery stalks, chopped into small chunks

1 onion, diced

2 cans water packed tuna, drained

salt

pepper

1 tsp chopped garlic

3 eggs

1 cup milk

4 oz Romano cheese

1 cup all-purpose flour

3 cups plain bread crumbs, lightly seasoned with salt, pepper, and Romano cheese

In a large bowl, combine the potatoes, celery, onion, tuna, salt, pepper, garlic, and Romano cheese with 1 of the eggs. Mix well. After mixing, form the mixture into small patties. Combine the milk and remaining eggs, and beat together. Dip one patty at a time into the flour, then into the beaten eggs, then into the bread crumbs. In a skillet, over medium heat, fry one side of the patty for 5 minutes, then turn it over and fry the other side for 3 minutes. Remove from heat, but keep warm. Serve with hot tomato sauce.

Serves 4-6

Buon Appetito!

Funghi ripieni
(Stuffed Mushrooms)

20 medium mushrooms, stems removed, chopped

3 tbsp butter or margarine

3 tbsp olive oil

1 garlic clove, minced

2 tbsp fresh chopped parsley

½ tsp salt

¼ tsp black pepper

¼ tsp dried oregano

¼ tsp dried basil

1 cup plain bread crumbs

½ cup Romano cheese

3 slices of mozzarella cheese, cut into small pieces to fit mushroom caps

Place the butter and oil in a medium frying pan, over medium heat. When the butter is melted, add the chopped mushroom stems, and cook for 4 minutes. Remove from heat. Mix in the garlic, parsley, salt, pepper, oregano, basil, bread crumbs, and Romano cheese. Stuffing is complete when all of the ingredients are mixed well. Spoon 1 tablespoon of the mixture into each mushroom cap. Cover each with one small piece of mozzarella cheese. When all of the caps are filled and covered with mozzarella, place them onto a greased, shallow baking dish. Bake uncovered at 375 degrees for 25 minutes, or until cheese is lightly browned.

Makes 5 servings (4 caps each)

Buon Appetito!

Polpettine di spinach e ricotta
(Spinach and Ricotta Patties)

2 ½ cups ricotta cheese
2 cups cooked spinach, chopped and drained well
1 egg
1 cup Romano cheese
2 cups flour, seasoned with salt and pepper

Combine the spinach, ricotta, egg, and Romano cheese, and mix very well. Heat some olive oil in a medium frying pan. Shape one tablespoon of the mixture into a ball; roll each ball into the flour. Gently drop 4 balls at a time into the hot oil, and fry until golden. Gently lift polpettine out of the oil with a slotted spoon. Place on a plate lined with paper towels to soak up the extra oil. Sprinkle polpettine with Romano cheese and serve hot with marinara sauce.

Buon Appetito!

Bagno di calcioffe e spinach
(Artichoke and Spinach Dip Appetizer)

1 (16 oz) can artichokes
1 small bag of fresh spinach
4 or 5 heads of green onion
1 (8 oz) container sour cream
8 oz Romano cheese
pinch of salt
pinch of pepper
¼ cup olive oil
Italian bread

Drain the artichokes, and place them in a food processor for 4-5 pulses.
In a medium sauce pan, add the artichokes, spinach, onion, oil, salt, and pepper.
Cook for about 10 minutes on medium heat. Remove from stove and add the sour cream. Mix well, add Romano cheese, and continue mixing well.
Serve hot with thinly sliced, warm Italian bread.

Buon Appetito!

Formaggio fresco in carrozza
(Fresh Cheese Appetizer)

8 slices of Italian bread
8 oz fresh Mozzarella cheese, cut into slices
¾ cup milk
2 eggs
salt and pepper to taste
½ cup butter

Trim the crust from the bread. Cut the cheese into 4 slices.
Place one slice of cheese on each slice of bread. Cover with a second slice of bread.
In a bowl, whip the eggs, milk, salt, and pepper.
In a large frying pan, melt the butter. Dip each sandwich into the batter, and cook for two minutes on each side, or until golden brown. Remove from the pan, cut into quarters and serve hot.

Serves 6

Buon Appetito!

Polipo con salsa di aceto
(Octopus with Vinegar Sauce)

2 lbs octopus, cleaned
10 fresh mint leaves
¼ cup wine vinegar
1 tsp sugar
4 garlic cloves, chopped
½ cup olive oil
1/3 cup water
½ tsp salt
¼ tsp pepper

In a large pot, boil the octopus for 20 minutes. Drain the hot water, and let it cool.
Rinse the octopus under cold water, rubbing off the skin as much as possible. Slice the octopus into small pieces (1 inch in length) and set them aside. In a small bowl, mix the vinegar, water, sugar, and mint, and set aside. Sautée the garlic in olive oil until golden. Set it aside and let cool. Next, pour in the vinegar mixture. Cover the pot, and bring it to a boil. Remove from heat. Pour the mixture over the octopus and mix well. Refrigerate for 3 hours before serving.

Serves 4

Buon Appetito!

Fritto di calamari
(Fried calamari)

2 lbs squid
1 cup all-purpose flour
1 cup plain bread crumbs
3 large eggs
1 cup milk
1 tsp salt
1 tsp pepper
1 tsp garlic
2 cups olive oil for frying
4 oz Romano cheese

Clean the squid, and cut it into ½ inch rings. Mix the bread crumbs, Romano cheese, salt, and pepper in a medium-sized bowl. Place the flour in a separate bowl. Mix the eggs and milk in a small bowl. In a medium frying pan, pour oil to about 1 inch depth. Heat the oil to 350 degrees (test the temperature with an oil thermometer).

Coat the squid rings with the flour, eggs, milk mixture, and finally, bread crumbs. Be sure to coat all the squid before beginning to fry. Have a cover ready for the frying pan; oil tends to splatter when frying the calamari. Cook the squid for 1 minute. Do not over cook, as the calamari will become tough.

Serves 6

Buon Appetito!

Broccoli Frittata

½ medium onion, julienne
1 bunch of fresh broccoli, cut into florets
4 oz good Romano cheese
¼ cup milk
¼ cup shredded mozzarella cheese
2 tbsp butter
¼ cup olive oil
1 small garlic clove, crushed
1 cup cooked white rice
½ tsp salt
6 eggs
1 dash pepper
1 (1 qt) casserole dish, buttered

Boil the broccoli for 5 minutes. Sautée the onion in melted butter and olive oil, until tender. Add the broccoli, garlic, rice, and Romano cheese. Mix well. Beat the eggs, milk, salt, and pepper together. Stir the beaten eggs into the rice and broccoli mixture. Pour that mixture into a well-buttered casserole dish. Top with shredded mozzarella cheese.

Bake at 350 degrees for 30 minutes. Make sure the casserole is set before serving.

Serves 4

Buon appetito!

Frittata di patate e calcioffe
(Potato and Artichoke Frittata)

1 (16 oz) can sliced artichokes in water

4 medium potatoes, peeled and sliced into 1/8 inch slices

1 medium onion, sliced

1 tsp salt

1 tsp pepper

6 large eggs, beaten

4 oz grated Romano cheese

6 oz olive oil

2 tbsp butter

In a large non-stick frying pan, pour the oil and butter. Add the potatoes, and cook over medium heat for 5 minutes. Add the onions and artichokes, and cook for 10 minutes longer. Add the salt and pepper. In a large bowl, beat the eggs. Add ½ teaspoon of salt, ¼ teaspoon of pepper, and the Romano cheese. Mix well, and set aside. Pour the egg mixture on top of the potatoes, cover the pan, and let it cook for 5 minutes. Gently shake the pan once to allow the eggs to settle better over the potatoes. Cover the frying pan with a large round plate, flip the frittata onto the plate, then gently slide it back into the pan. Cook for 2 minutes longer. Remove from the stove, and slide back onto a clean plate. Serve hot or cold.

Serves 4

Buon Appetito!

Arancine
(Sicilian Rice Ball)

2 cups rice
2 cups grated Romano cheese
1 tsp salt
½ tsp pepper
1 cup flour, seasoned with salt and pepper
4 eggs, beaten
¼ cup milk
2 cups bread crumbs, seasoned with salt,
    pepper, and 2 oz Romano cheese

oil for frying

Filling -
½ lb ground beef
2 tbsp olive oil
1 cup frozen peas
2 tbsp finely chopped parsley
1 onion, finely chopped
1 cup crushed tomato
2 garlic cloves, minced
¼ tsp dry oregano
½ tsp dry basil
¼ tsp salt
¼ tsp pepper

Rice
Cook the rice in 7 cups of water. Bring to a boil, reduce heat, and simmer until soft and all the water is absorbed. The rice will be sticky. Add 2 cups of Romano cheese to the rice, and mix very well. Remove the pot from the stove, cover, and let cool.

Filling
In a medium frying pan, add the oil, onion, and garlic. Sautée until soft. Add the ground beef, salt, pepper, oregano, and basil, and cook until the ground beef is no longer pink. Add the crushed tomatoes and cook for 10 minutes longer. Drain the fat from the meat and let it cool.

Forming the rice ball
Weigh 4 ounces of rice for each ball. In a small bowl, pour ¼ cup of oil to dip your hands into. Roll the 4 ounces of rice in the palms of your hands to form a ball. With two fingers, push the center of the rice ball very gently until you have an opening big enough to put a tablespoon of the meat mixture into. Gently start closing the opening until you have a ball again.

Frying
Put oil in a pot high enough to cover 2 or 3 rice balls. Let the oil get hot at a low temperature. In the meantime, first, roll the rice balls in the flour. Second, roll them in the beaten eggs. Last, roll them in the bread crumbs. Before you start frying, have all of the rice balls ready.
Fry them for 3 minutes, or until they are golden brown. Remove them with a slotted spoon. Drain onto paper towels.

Serves 6

Buon Appetito!

Vongale al forno
(Baked Stuffed Clams)

12 clams, well cleaned
2 tbsp butter
3 tbsp olive oil
1 garlic clove, minced
1 tbsp fresh parsley
1 tsp dried oregano
2 tbsp good Romano cheese
¼ cup onion, finely chopped
1 cup plain bread crumbs
¼ tsp salt
¼ tsp pepper
3 cups water

In a medium skillet, heat the oil and butter. Add the onion, garlic, parsley, oregano, salt, pepper, and bread crumbs. Cook together for 2 minutes, and then remove from heat. Add the Romano cheese to the mixture.

In a medium pot, place the clams in 3 cups of water. Cover and let simmer on medium heat, until the clams open--about 5-10 minutes. Allow the clams to cool for 15 minutes, or until cool enough to touch. Open the clams in half. Fill the half containing the clam with one teaspoon of the bread crumb mixture. Bake at 400 degrees for 10 minutes, or broil 5 inches from the heat for only 3 to 4 minutes. Serve with lemon wedges.

Makes 12 clam halves

Buon Appetito!

SOUPS

Zuppa a minestra
(Vegetable and Beef Minestrone Soup)

¼ lb ground beef

1 head of celery

4 garlic cloves, minced

1 medium onion

4 medium zucchini, cut in half and sliced ¼ inch thick

1 small green pepper, seeded and diced

2 medium carrots, peeled and sliced into rounds

1 small head of cabbage, cleaned and sliced into small chunks

1½ tsp salt

½ tsp pepper

¼ tsp dried oregano

¼ tsp dry basil

4 cups beef stock

1 (12 oz) can tomato purée

½ cup olive oil

In a large sauce pot, sautée the onion and garlic over medium heat for 2 minutes, stirring often. Add the ground beef and cook for 4 minutes, stirring often. Add the zucchini, celery, carrots, cabbage, green peppers, salt, pepper, oregano, basil, beef stock, tomato purée, and 4 cups of water.

Let the mixture come to a full boil, lower the heat, and simmer for 15 minutes, or until the carrots are soft. Add more water if needed.

Serves 6-8

Buon Appetito!

Pasta e Fagioli con Polppettine di Carne

(Pasta and Fagioli Soup with Small Meatballs)

3 (16 oz) cans cannelloni beans or navy beans

5 garlic cloves, minced

2 tbsp salt

1 tsp pepper

1 tsp crushed red pepper

4 tomatoes, cleaned, seeded and diced

1 tsp dried oregano

1 tsp dried basil

1 small carrot, shredded

1 egg

2 oz whipping cream

2 cups ditalini pasta

¼ cup olive oil

1 large onion, finely chopped

4 celery stalks, thinly sliced

4 sprigs parsley, chopped

½ lb ground beef, 80/20

½ cup bread crumbs

½ cup grated Romano cheese, plus more for sprinkling

In a bowl, combine the ground beef, egg, bread crumbs, whipping cream, cheese, and a pinch of the salt and pepper. Mix it all together. Take a teaspoon full of the mixture and roll it into a ball. Continue for the rest of the ground beef. In a large frying pan, heat the olive oil over medium heat. Cook meatballs until they are golden brown, 2-3 minutes on each side. Remove them from heat and set them aside. In the same frying pan, add the garlic and onions, and sautée until they are a light golden color. Transfer the onions and garlic into a large soup pot. Add the celery, carrots, tomatoes, remaining salt and pepper, crushed red pepper, oregano, basil, and 3 cans of beef stock. Bring to a boil over medium-high heat for 5 minutes. Cover, turn heat to low and simmer for 30 minutes, stirring often. If needed, add water. There should be enough liquid to cook the ditalini. When the carrots are almost soft, add the ditalini. Cook for an additional 8 minutes. Add the meatballs that have been set aside and simmer 3 minutes more. Remove from heat. Serve immediately, sprinkled with Romano cheese.

Serves 6

Buon Appetito!

Zuppa di melenzane e pomodori arrostiti
(Roasted Eggplant, Garlic and Tomato Bisque)

1 small onion, chopped
2 garlic cloves, chopped
2 medium eggplants, cut in half, and peeled
5 small tomatoes, cut in half, seeds removed
2 cups chicken stock
1 ½ cups whipping cream
½ tsp white pepper
1 tbsp salt
4 oz Romano cheese
¼ cup olive oil

Lay the eggplants and tomatoes onto a baking sheet, with the sliced ends facing down. Brush them with olive oil, and season with salt and pepper. Roast the eggplants and tomatoes at 400 degrees for 30 minutes. Check for softness of the eggplant with a fork. If needed, bake for 15 minutes longer. Remove them from the oven and let cool for 15 minutes. Once cooled, remove the skin from the tomatoes, and the seeds from the eggplants. Process the tomatoes and the eggplants in a food processor for 10 seconds. Scoop the mixture into a bowl and set it aside. In a medium pot heat olive oil over medium heat. Add onion and garlic and sautee for 2 minutes. Add the eggplants and tomatoes to the onion and garlic, and mix together. Cook over low heat for 5 minutes, stirring often. Add the chicken stock and simmer for 5 minutes. Add the whipping cream and Romano cheese, stirring really well. Remove from heat.

Serves 4

Buon Appetito!

Zuppa di Pisellini Verde
(Split Pea Soup)

4 cups dried split peas

2 cups chicken stock

4 cups water

4 slices ham, 1 inch thick, cubed

2 cups broccoli florets

1 onion, chopped

1 head of celery, chopped

2 carrots, peeled and sliced

1 tbsp salt

½ tsp pepper

½ tsp hot red pepper flakes

1 garlic clove, chopped

¼ cup olive oil

In a large sauce pot, combine the olive oil, onion, and garlic. Sautée over medium heat for 2 minutes. Add the rest of the ingredients, except for the ham. Cook for 45 minutes, then add the ham. Cook for 30 minutes longer.
Serve sprinkled with Romano cheese.

Serves 8

Buon Appetito!

Zuppa di pomodori
(Tomato Soup)

1 onion, chopped

3 tbsp olive oil

1 (16 oz) can crushed tomatoes

1 (8 oz) can tomato sauce

1 ½ cups chicken stock

4 fresh basil leaves, cut in half

1 tsp fresh thyme

In a medium sauce pot, combine the olive oil, onion, and garlic. Sautée until onions are tender. Add the crushed tomatoes, tomato sauce, chicken stock, basil, thyme, salt, and pepper. Cook for 30 minutes on low heat. Transfer the soup into a food processor. Process until smooth, then return to the sauce pot. Simmer on low heat until the soup boils.
Serve sprinkled with Romano cheese, along with crusty Italian bread.

Serves 4

Buon Appetito!

Zuppa di broccoli e patate
(Broccoli and Potato Soup)

3 large potatoes, peeled and cubed
3 cups fresh broccoli florets
1 medium onion, finely chopped
1 garlic clove, minced
1 tbsp butter
¼ cup olive oil
3¼ cups milk
½ cup heavy cream
1 cup chicken broth
¼ cup Romano cheese
10 oz Velveeta cheese, cut into small pieces
½ tsp pepper
1 tbsp salt

In a large sauce pot, sautée the potatoes, onions, and garlic in the olive oil and butter until the onions are tender. Add the broccoli, chicken broth, and milk. Cover and let it cook on medium heat until the potatoes are tender—about 20 minutes. Add the salt, pepper, heavy cream, Velveeta cheese, and Romano cheese. Stir frequently until the cheese is melted.

Serves 6

Buon Appetito!

Zuppa di gallina con crema
(Chicken Soup in White Cream Sauce)

1 onion
1 cup mushrooms, sliced
1 (10 oz) bag of frozen peas
1 (10 oz) bag of frozen carrots
½ cup butter
2/3 cup flour
1 tsp salt
1 tsp oregano
½ tsp pepper
4 cups chicken broth
2 cups whole milk
6 cups fresh chicken, cubed
2 parsley sprigs, finely chopped

In a medium pot, pour 8 cups of water, and bring to a boil over medium heat. Add the chicken, cover, and let it cook for 20 minutes. Remove the chicken with a slotted spoon. Set it aside and keep warm. Save 5 cups of the broth.

In a large pot, over medium heat, melt the butter. Add the flour, stirring quickly until a paste is formed. Add 4 cups of the broth, stirring until the butter and flour are dissolved. Add the mushrooms, peas, carrots, oregano, salt, and pepper, and simmer for about 20 minutes, or until the carrots are soft when pricked with a fork. Add the chicken and milk and cook for an additional 10 minutes. If needed, add a little more broth. Serve immediately.

Serves 6

Buon Appetito!

SAUCES

Marinara Sauce

2 16oz cans of crushed tomatoes
1 large white onion, chopped
6 garlic cloves, chopped
1/4 cup parsley, chopped
1/2 cup olive oil
10 fresh basil leaves, cut in half
1 tsp dried basil
1 tsp black pepper
1 tbsp salt
1/4 tsp baking soda
1 tbsp sugar
1/4 cup dry white wine
1 cup water

Heat olive oil in a medium sauce pot. Over medium heat, sautée onion, garlic, parsley, and basil until onions are tender. Add the 2 cans of crushed tomatoes, one cup of water, salt, pepper, sugar, baking soda and dried basil. Bring to a boil, lower the heat and simmer for about 30 minutes, stirring often so sauce does not burn. When finished cooking add the wine, stir and remove from heat. Use immediately over your favorite dish or store in Mason jars or other airtight container. Marinara sauce will keep in the refrigerator for 7 days.

Buon Appetito!

Sugo di Pomodori
(Tomato Sauce)

2 16 oz cans of tomato puree

1 16 oz can of crushed tomatoes

1 cup cold water

1 large yellow onion, chopped

2 garlic cloves, minced

1/2 tsp garlic powder

1 tsp dried oregano

1 tsp salt

1/2 tsp black pepper

1/2 tsp sugar

1/4 tsp baking soda

1/2 cup olive oil

6 sprigs of parsley, finely chopped

6 basil leaves, cut in half

1 large carrot (optional)

4 celery stalks (optional)

In a food processor, process carrot and celery until a paste is formed.

In a large sauce pot, heat olive oil over medium heat. Sautee onions and garlic until onions are translucent. Add carrots, celery, parsley and basil and sautee for 5 minutes. Add the tomato puree, the crushed tomatoes and the water. Add the baking soda, mix well. Cook for about 15 minutes. Add the salt, pepper, dried oregano, and sugar and cook for an additional 15 minutes. Sauce will be ready in 30 minutes. Serve immediately over your favorite pasta or store in Mason jars or other airtight container. Sauce will keep in the refrigerator for 7 days.

Buon Appetito!

Alfredo Sauce

3 egg yolks
5 cups heavy whipping cream
2 tsp fresh parsley, chopped
1/2 tsp butter
1/8 tsp salt
1/8 tsp white pepper
2 cups Romano cheese, grated plus more for sprinkling

In a medium mixing bowl combine cream and egg yolks. Whisk together and add 2 cups of the Romano cheese until well blended.
In a large skillet over medium heat combine butter, cream mixture, parsley, salt and pepper. Stir constantly until thickened. Serve immediately over fettucine or your favorite pasta.

Serves 4.

Buon Appetito!

Sugo di Melenzane

(Eggplant sauce)

2 medium eggplants
1 cup olive oil
2 16oz can of chopped tomatoes
1 medium yellow onion, chopped
4 garlic cloves, chopped
1 tbsp salt
1 tsp black pepper
1/4 tsp baking soda
1 tbsp sugar
1/4 cup capers
1 cup kalamata olives, pitted
1/4 cup fresh basil, chopped
Romano cheese for sprinkling

Wash and peel eggplants. Remove stems, cut eggplant lengthwise into 1 inch thick slices, then into cubes. In a large frying pan heat ½ cup of olive oil over medium heat. Begin frying the eggplant by slowly placing small batches into the hot oil. Fry until eggplants are a golden color on all sides. Remove from oil, drain on paper towels.

In a medium sauce pot, heat the remaining ½ cup of olive oil over medium heat. Add onion and garlic and sautee for 2 minutes. Add chopped tomatoes, salt, pepper, baking soda, sugar, capers, olives and 8oz cold water. Bring to a boil. Lower the heat and simmer for 30 minutes. Add eggplant and fresh basil and simmer for 5 minutes longer. Remove from heat and serve immediately over your favorite pasta, sprinkled with Romano cheese. Any leftover sauce will keep in the refrigerator for 7 days.

Buon Appetito!

Vongale in Sugo Bianco
(White Clam Sauce)

1 (32 oz) can clams (do not drain)
2 cups milk
1 medium onion, chopped
4 garlic cloves, chopped
4 tbsp butter
½ cup flour
½ tsp oregano
½ tsp salt
½ tsp pepper
2 tbsp fresh parsley, finely chopped
2 oz white wine
½ cup Romano cheese

In a medium sauce pot, sautée onion and garlic in butter, until tender. Stir in the flour, oregano, salt, and pepper. Add the milk and clams (juice included), and cook until thick and bubbling.
Stir in the parsley and wine, and simmer for 1 minute more.
Pour clam sauce over your favorite pasta.

Serves 6

Buon Appetito!

Ravioli Carbonara

24 ravioli, meat or cheese

5 scallions, chopped

6 slices of pancetta (or bacon if you can't find pancetta) , cut into 1 ½ inch pieces, cooked crispy

2 cups fresh sliced mushrooms

2 tbsp butter

1 ½ tbsp salt

¼ tsp white pepper

32 oz heavy cream

16 oz grated Pecorino Romano cheese

Fill a large pot ¾ full with water. Bring the water to a boil and add salt and the ravioli. Cook until the ravioli float, and are soft to the touch.

In a small frying pan, over medium heat, combine 1 tablespoon of the butter with the scallions, mushrooms, and pancetta. Sauté until the onions are soft. Remove from heat and set aside.

In a large pot, combine the cream and remaining butter. Cook on low heat, stirring often, for about five minutes, and then add the scallion/mushroom/pancetta mixture. Add the Romano cheese. Be sure to keep stirring often until the mixture becomes a thick cream--about 7-8 minutes. Cook's tip: Sauce is ready when the stirring spoon stays coated with cream sauce.

Pour cream sauce over plated ravioli and serve immediately.

Serves 6

Buon Appetito!

Gamberi fra diavolo
(Spicy Shrimp and Linguini)

1 white onion
2 tsp chopped garlic
4 fresh basil leaves
½ tsp fresh parsley
¼ tsp salt
1/8 tsp black pepper
1 tsp crushed red pepper
2 (8 oz) cans tomato sauce
3 tbsp olive oil
¼ cup cognac or brandy
14 shrimp, peeled, de-veined, tails removed

In a medium pot, over medium heat, sautée the onion, garlic, basil, and parsley until the onion is translucent. Add both cans of tomato sauce, ¼ cup of water, and the salt, pepper, and crushed red pepper. Cook for about 8 minutes over medium heat. Add the shrimp and cognac or brandy, and cook for 5 minutes longer. Make sure the shrimp are pink. Remove from heat and keep warm. Serve over cooked linguini and sprinkle with Romano cheese.

Serves 4

Buon Appetito!

Insalata di Pollo
(Chicken Salad)

1 small bag of baby spinach

1 small head of Romaine lettuce, chopped

1 lb cooked chicken, cubed

1 large red onion, sliced

½ cup red pepper, julienne

1 small navel orange, pealed and sliced into small pieces

2 celery stalks, sliced

1 (8 oz) can pineapple, drained

1 oz red wine vinegar

2 tsp honey

½ cup olive oil

½ cup toasted pine nuts

¼ cup toasted coconut flakes

salt and pepper to taste

¼ tsp dried oregano

¼ tsp dried basil

In a large salad bowl, combine the spinach, lettuce, chicken, onion, red peppers, orange,
celery, and pineapple. Mix well and set aside. In a jar, mix the oil, vinegar, honey, salt, pepper, oregano, and
basil. Shake well. Pour over the salad mixture. Top with pineapple and pine nuts.

Serves 6

Buon Appetito!

Insalata di melenzane

(Eggplant Salad)

2 eggplants, sliced

2 eggs, beaten

2 cups bread crumbs, seasoned with salt, pepper, parsley, and 2 oz Romano cheese

1 cup flour

¼ tsp salt

¼ tsp pepper

1 green pepper, cut into rings

1 yellow pepper, cut into rings

1 red onion, cut into rings

2 tbsp dry oregano

6 oz grated Romano cheese

½ cup red wine vinegar

oil for frying (about 3-4 cups)

Coat the eggplants with the flour. Next, dip them into the eggs. Afterward, dip them into the bread crumbs. Heat the oil in a Dutch oven. Place the eggplants into the hot oil. Once the eggplants are done, remove them from the oil, and drain onto paper towels. Layer the eggplants in a salad bowl. Next, layer the green peppers, yellow peppers, and onions. Sprinkle with Romano cheese, salt, pepper, oregano, and vinegar. Repeat for each layer.

Allow the salad to rest for 2 hours before serving.

Serves 4

Buon Appetito!

Osso buco Siciliano
(Veal Shanks - Sicilian Style)

6 veal shanks, cut 2 ½ inches thick

1 ½ cups olive oil

1 carrot, peeled and chopped

¾ cup dry white wine

¼ cup fresh parsley, chopped

5 celery stalks

1 tsp salt

1 tsp pepper

½ cup flour

1 medium onion, chopped

2 cans (16 oz) crushed tomatoes

4 garlic cloves, minced

fresh basil

Coat the veal with the flour. In a large frying pan, heat ½ cup of oil over medium heat. Add the veal and brown both sides. Remove them from the pan and set aside.

In a large pot, pour 1 cup of oil, the onion, carrots, celery, parsley, and garlic. Sautée for 10 minutes. Add the veal, wine, crushed tomato, salt, and pepper. Cover the pot, and simmer for 1½ hours. Veal will be ready when the meat falls from the bone.

Arrange the meat onto a platter garnished with basil leaves. This succulent dish is delicious served with risotto.

Serves 6

Buon Appetito!

Vongale al forno
(Baked Stuffed Clams)

12 clams, well cleaned
2 tbsp butter
3 tbsp olive oil
1 garlic clove, minced
1 tbsp fresh parsley
1 tsp dried oregano
2 tbsp good Romano cheese
¼ cup onion, finely chopped
1 cup plain bread crumbs
¼ tsp salt
¼ tsp pepper
3 cups water

In a medium skillet, heat the oil and butter. Add the onion, garlic, parsley, oregano, salt, pepper, and bread crumbs. Cook together for 2 minutes, and then remove from heat. Add the Romano cheese to the mixture.

In a medium pot, place the clams in 3 cups of water. Cover and let simmer on medium heat, until the clams open--about 5-10 minutes. Allow the clams to cool for 15 minutes, or until cool enough to touch. Open the clams in half. Fill the half containing the clam with one teaspoon of the bread crumb mixture. Bake at 400 degrees for 10 minutes, or broil 5 inches from the heat for only 3 to 4 minutes. Serve with lemon wedges.

Makes 12 clam halves

Buon Appetito!

Panelle

3 ½ cups water
2 cups garbanzo bean flour
2 tsp salt
3 cups olive oil
Good quality Italian bread
black pepper to taste
lemons

In a medium pot, pour the water, salt, pepper, and flour. Whisk to avoid lumps. Cook over medium heat, stirring constantly. The mixture will get thick; keep on stirring until you see the bottom of the pan, and the spoon stands in the center of the pot.

Remove from heat, and pour the mixture onto a clean, flat surface, like a wooden block or table. Use a spatula dipped in oil to QUICKLY spread the mixture to ¼ inch thickness. Let panelle cool for ten minutes, then cut it into squares.

In a large frying pan, heat two inches of oil. Carefully place panelle in the pan (oil will be hot). Fry until golden and slightly puffy. Drain panelle on a paper towel. Place panelle onto good Italian bread. Add a little lemon juice, salt, and pepper to taste.

Serves 6

Buon Appetito!

Vitellino con Marsala
(Veal Marsala)

4 veal cutlets, pounded thin
2 tbsp fresh parsley, chopped
1 cup marsala wine
1 cup olive oil
½ cup beef broth
1 ½ cups bread crumbs
½ cup grated Romano cheese
1 small onion, cut in half and thinly sliced
¼ cup milk
1 egg, beaten
¼ lb sliced mushrooms
1 tbsp salt
1 tsp pepper
1 garlic clove, minced
1 cup flour
1 (8 oz) can whole artichoke hearts

Drain the artichokes, and cut each artichoke heart into 6 pieces. In a small bowl, mix the egg and milk. Put the flour into a second small bowl. In a third bowl, mix the bread crumbs, 1 tablespoon of the fresh parsley, Romano cheese, salt, and pepper. In a medium frying pan, pour ¼ cup of olive oil. Add the mushrooms, parsley, onion, garlic, and artichokes. Sautée for 5 minutes, and set aside.

To fry veal cutlets, first, coat the veal with flour, then with eggs, and last, with bread crumbs. Set it aside. Pour the remaining oil into a large frying pan, and turn the heat to medium. Make sure the oil is hot before frying the veal. Fry the veal cutlets until they are golden brown on both sides. In a non-stick baking pan, set the veal cutlets side by side. Place the mushroom and artichoke mixture on top of the cutlets. Mix the marsala and broth together, and pour it over the cutlets.

Bake at 450 degrees for 10 minutes.
Serve with pasta or garlic mashed potatoes and a green salad.

Serves 4

Buon Appetito!

Piatto del Marinaio
(Seafood Platter)

3 tbsp olive oil

2 large garlic cloves, minced

2 large portabella mushrooms, thinly sliced

1 small onion, finely chopped

4 oz small scallops

12 shrimp, cleaned and de-veined

3 calamari (squid), cut into rings

6 mussels, cleaned

4 oz lobster meat, cut into chunks

2 cans artichoke hearts, drained and cut into small pieces

1 package sun dried tomatoes, julienne

1 tsp salt (or enough salt to taste)

½ tsp freshly ground white pepper

1½ lbs capellini pasta, cooked

8 small clams

In a large skillet, heat the oil over low heat. Add the garlic, stirring until it is golden brown. Be sure not to brown the garlic too much, as this will make it bitter. Add the mushrooms, and cook for 2 to 3 minutes. Stir in the seafood, artichoke hearts, sun dried tomatoes, and clams. Cook for 5 to 6 minutes, or until the clams are open. Add salt and pepper.

Pour the seafood over cooked capellini, sprinkle with grated Romano cheese, and serve!

Serves 4

Buon Appetito!

Imbottini di prosciutto a formaggio
(Prosciutto and Mozzarella Sandwich)

8 thin slices of good Italian bread, trimmed of crust
4 slices mozzarella cheese
8 slices prosciutto
1 cup milk
2 ½ cup all-purpose flour
6 eggs, lightly beaten
½ cup olive oil
3 tbsp butter
3 tsp fresh lemon juice
½ tsp anchovy paste (optional)

Assemble the sandwiches. Place 1 slice of bread, 1 slice of cheese, 2 slices of prosciutto and top it off with another slice of bread. Cut the sandwich into halves. Pour the milk into a small bowl, the eggs into another bowl, and the flour into a third bowl. In a medium frying pan, heat the oil. In the meantime, coat each andwich with milk first, then flour, and then eggs. Brown 2 sandwiches at a time, turning once. Sandwiches are ready when they have a golden brown color. Remove them from the pan and place them on a plate to keep warm. In a small frying pan, melt the butter over medium-high heat. Stir in the anchovy paste and lemon juice. Blend well, and drizzle it over the sandwiches. Serve immediately.

Serves 4

Buon Appetito!

Veal Spiedini

18 fresh bay leaves

12 veal slices (veal slices for scalloping work well)

½ cup olive oil

1 small onion, finely chopped

½ cup grated Romano cheese

¼ cup pine nuts

12 thin slices of Genoa salami, cut into small pieces

12 thin slices of prosciutto, cut into small pieces

1 cup golden raisins

2 ½ cups bread crumbs

2 eggs, beaten

6 cherry tomatoes, each cut into 4 pieces

(Soak raisins in warm water for half an hour.)

In a large frying pan, heat 2 tablespoons of oil. Add the onions, and cook until translucent. Add the bread crumbs and 2 more tablespoons of oil. Mix thoroughly, and cook for 2 minutes longer. Remove from heat, add cheese, raisins, pine nuts, salami, prosciutto, tomato, salt, and pepper. Mix very well. Place a spoonful of stuffing on each slice of veal. Roll the meat and secure it with a toothpick.

Dip the rolls of veal into the eggs, then into the rest of the bread crumbs. Double-skewer each veal roll. Drizzle olive oil onto the veal rolls. Place the veal rolls on the grill for 8 minutes on each side, drizzling oil as needed. Suggested served with Polpettine de patate and a salad.

Serves 4

Buon Appetito!

Pollo del Cacciatore

(Chicken Cacciatore)

1 chicken, cut in half, with each half cut into 4 pieces

1 medium onion, julienne

2 garlic cloves, chopped

1 cup mushrooms, sliced

1 green pepper, seeds removed, julienne

4 tbsp olive oil plus 1/4 cup

¼ cup dry white wine

¼ tsp basil

¼ tsp oregano

½ tsp salt

½ tsp pepper

¼ tsp red pepper flakes

½ cup sliced black olives

2 cups marinara sauce

Place the chicken in a 13x9 glass dish and drizzle 1/4 cup of olive oil on the chicken. Bake at 400 degrees, uncovered, for 45 minutes. Remove the chicken from the oven and set it aside. Heat the olive oil in an extra large skillet. Add the onion and garlic, and cook for 2 minutes. Add the mushrooms, green pepper, and olives. Sautée together for 3 minutes. Add the marinara sauce and wine, and cook for a few minutes longer. Add the baked chicken to the pan, making sure to cover the chicken with sauce. Cover the pan and let the chicken cook for 5 more minutes. Uncover, sprinkle with ¼ teaspoon of red pepper flakes, and mix well. Cover, remove from the heat, and set it aside for 5 minutes. Best served with a side of farfalle pasta.

Serves 6

Buon Appetito!

Gamberi al Forno
(Baked Shrimp)

12 jumbo shrimp
2 eggs, beaten
½ cup parsley, chopped
2 cups plain bread crumbs
2 cloves garlic, chopped
½ cup olive oil
1 cup flour
½ cup Romano cheese
½ tsp salt
dash of pepper

Combine the bread crumbs, salt, pepper, and cheese into a bowl.
One at a time, coat the shrimp first in flour, then egg, then bread crumbs.
Place the shrimp on a baking dish well coated with olive oil. Drizzle the remaining oil over the shrimp. Bake at 400 degrees for 20 minutes, or until golden brown. Do not over cook! Serve hot.

Suggested paired with a tomato, red onion, and fresh basil salad. Combine the salad ingredients, sprinkle with oregano, salt and pepper, and drizzle with olive oil.

Serves 2

Buon Appetito!

Pollo Alla Tetrazzini
(Chicken Tetrazzini)

6 chicken breasts, each cut into 4 sections

1 large garlic clove, minced

2 cups heavy cream

5 tbsp butter

1 cup grated Romano cheese

½ tsp salt

¼ tsp white pepper

3 cups thick sliced mushrooms

1 lb spaghetti, cooked al dente

¼ cup sherry

In a medium sauce pot, bring 8 cups of water to a boil. Season the chicken with salt and pepper, and place it into the pot. Cook for 30 minutes, remove, and set aside. Save 2 cups of the chicken broth. In a medium frying pan, add 3 tablespoons of butter along with the garlic. Sautée for 1 minute, and add the flour and chicken broth, stirring constantly until the sauce is creamy. Add the sherry, blending well with the cream sauce.
In a small sauce pan, melt the remaining butter, and add the mushrooms, salt, and pepper. Sautée for 4 minutes over medium heat. Remove from heat. Butter a large baking pan. Add the spaghetti, chicken, mushroom, cream sauce, and ½ cup of Romano cheese. Mix well. Sprinkle the remaining cheese on top. Bake at 475 degrees for 10 minutes.

Serve 4

Buon Appetito!

Vitello Alla Pizzaiola
(Veal Chops Pizzaiola)

8 veal chops, ½ inch thick
2 (16 oz) cans crushed tomato
1 tsp dried basil
½ tsp dried oregano
2 sprigs parsley, chopped
4 garlic cloves, sliced
3 tbsp Romano cheese
1 tbsp salt
1 tsp pepper
1 small yellow onion, chopped
1 cup beef broth
½ cup olive oil

In a large frying pan, heat ¼ cup of the olive oil. Brown the veal chops on both sides, and set them aside. In a Dutch oven, add the remaining olive oil, onion, garlic, salt, and pepper, and sautée for 3 minutes. Add the crushed tomato, oregano, basil, and parsley. Bring to a boil, and add beef broth, stirring well. Add the veal chops, reduce the heat, cover, and cook for 1 hour. Chops are done when they are fork tender. Suggested served over fettuccini and sprinkled with Romano cheese.

Serves 4

Buon Appetito!

Capellini Pasta con Pollo Pizzaiola
(Angel Hair Pasta with Chicken Pizzaiola)

4 chicken breasts

1 lb angel hair pasta

1 large yellow onion, sliced

1 (12 oz) bag of frozen peas

½ cup Romano cheese

1 lb mushrooms, sliced

1 (16 oz) can crushed tomatoes

1 (16 oz) can tomato purée

2 garlic cloves

1 tsp salt

½ tsp pepper

¼ cup olive oil

In a large pan, sautée the onion and garlic in the olive oil for 3 minutes. Add the chicken breasts, and cook for 5 minutes, turning the chicken once. Add the mushrooms, tomato purée, and crushed tomatoes. Bring it to a boil. Add the salt, pepper, and 10 ounces of water. Reduce the heat, cover, and cook until the chicken is tender, stirring often.

Cook the angel hair according to package directions. Drain the pasta. Place it onto 4 dinner plates. Place 1 piece of chicken breast on top of the pasta, and ladle one scoop of the sauce over the pasta and chicken. Sprinkle with Romano cheese.

Serves 4

Buon Appetito!

Pasta con carne
(Pasta with Strip Steak)

2 lbs strip steak, cubed

1 ½ cups beef broth

2 sprigs parsley, chopped

4 tbsp olive oil

2 cups fresh mushrooms, sliced

1 medium yellow onion, chopped

4 garlic cloves, minced

¼ cup flour

1 small green pepper, chopped

1 (12 oz) can tomato purée

¼ tsp thyme

¼ tsp fresh rosemary

4 fresh basil leaves, cut into four pieces

½ tsp salt

¼ tsp pepper

½ cup Romano cheese

Combine the flour and strip steak in a bowl, and toss to coat. In a frying pan, brown the meat on all sides. Remove the meat with a slotted spoon and set it aside. In the same frying pan, add the mushrooms, onion, garlic, and green pepper. Cook for 5 minutes. Add the beef broth, tomato purée, salt, pepper, basil, rosemary, thyme, and cooked steak. Cook for 45 minutes. If needed, add a little water.
Suggested served over linguini, sprinkled with a little Romano cheese.

Serves 4

Buon Appetito!

Melenzane Parmigiana
(Eggplant Parmigiana)

2 large eggplants

6 eggs, beaten

1 cup milk

3 cups bread crumbs

1 cup Romano cheese

2 tbsp fresh parsley, chopped

2 cups all-purpose flour

2 tsp salt

1 tsp pepper

3 cups olive oil

1 lb mozzarella cheese, shredded

For sauce:
Refer to the sauce recipe on page 30.

Remove the eggplant ends and slice them into ¼ inch thick rounds.
Beat the eggs and milk together.
Preheat the oven to 400 degrees.
In a large bowl, combine the bread crumbs, ½ cup of Romano cheese, 1 teaspoon of salt, 1 teaspoon of pepper, and the parsley. Pour the flour into a shallow dish, and add the remaining salt. Place the oil in a large frying pan over low heat. Dip the eggplants into the flour. Next, dip them into the eggs and then into the bread crumbs. Repeat until all of the eggplant slices are breaded. Turn the heat up to medium-high. Start frying 3 to 4 slices at a time. Continue until all of the eggplants are fried. Set them aside.

Place a scoop of the sauce onto a large baking pan, and arrange all the pieces of eggplant on top of the sauce. Add more sauce on top of the eggplant. Next, sprinkle Romano cheese and shredded mozzarella cheese on top of the eggplants. Bake until the cheese is melted and has a golden color. Serve hot with a side of penne pasta.

Serves 4

Buon Appetito!

Pollo alla Parmigiana
(Chicken Parmigiana)

6 chicken cutlets

2 cups Italian seasoned bread crumbs

1 cup flour

1 tsp salt

½ tsp pepper

2 eggs, beaten

1 cup olive oil

32 oz marinara sauce

16 oz mozzarella cheese, shredded

Heat the olive oil in a large frying pan over low heat. Place the bread crumbs in a bowl, the flour in another bowl, and the eggs in one more bowl. Dip the chicken first into the flour, then into the egg batter, and last, into the bread crumbs. Fry each cutlet for 5 minutes on each side, or until golden brown. Drain the cutlets on a paper towel, and set them aside. Pour 8 ounces of marinara sauce into a baking casserole. Layer the chicken on top of the sauce. Pour another 8 ounces of sauce on top of the cutlets, and cover them with the mozzarella cheese. Bake at 400 degrees until the cheese is melted and is a light golden color—about 10-15 minutes. Serve with angel hair pasta topped with the rest of the sauce.

Serves 6

Buon Appetito!

Lasagna al forno
(Baked Lasagna)

1 lb ground beef
½ lb bulk sausage
1 medium onion, chopped
2 garlic cloves, minced
1 tsp salt
½ tsp pepper
1 tsp dry basil
½ tsp dry oregano
2 sprigs parsley, chopped
¼ cup olive oil
1½ cups grated Romano cheese
1 lb mozzarella cheese, shredded
1 lb ricotta cheese - seasoned with ¼ tsp salt, ¼ tsp pepper, ½ cup Romano cheese, 1 tsp
    fresh parsley, and 1 egg (Mix well and set aside.)
1 lb of lasagna noodles - cooked according to package directions. Drain and rinse
    in cold water until noodles are cooled.

In a large frying pan, heat the olive oil. Sautée the onion and garlic until golden. Add the sausage to the pan, and cook for 3 minutes. Add the ground beef, and cook for another 5 minutes. Add the salt, pepper, and parsley, and cook for 2 minutes longer. Stir often, making sure to mix very well. When the meat is cooked through and no longer pink, remove from the heat and drain the fat. Set meat aside. In a 10 x 12 lasagna tray, add 2 ladles of tomato sauce to the bottom. Add ¼ cup of water, and mix well. Layer some noodles, lengthwise, on top of the sauce. Next, layer some meat the length of the pan. Layer the ricotta mixture on top of the meat. Cover with another layer of sauce. Sprinkle Romano cheese, and a layer of mozzarella cheese. Repeat for the second layer, this time layering noodles crosswise. Continue until the tray is filled. Finish with a layer of noodles. Cover with 2 scoops of sauce, a sprinkle of Romano cheese, and a layer of mozzarella cheese. Cover with aluminum foil and bake for 30 minutes at 400 degrees. For the last 5 minutes of baking, take the foil off and let the cheese brown lightly.

Serves 6

Buon Appetito!

Petti di Pollo con Prosciutto a Formaggio
(Chicken Saltimbocca)

6 boneless chicken breasts, pounded thin
½ cup flour
½ tsp salt
¼ tsp white pepper
¼ cup butter
½ cup olive oil
6 slices of good prosciutto
6 slices of good provolone cheese
¼ cup Romano cheese
¼ cup dry white wine

Mix the flour, salt, and pepper in a large bowl. Coat the chicken in the flour and set it aside. Heat the olive oil and butter in a large frying pan. Add the chicken, and sautée until the chicken is golden brown on both sides. Add the wine to the frying pan. Cover the chicken with one slice of prosciutto and one slice of provolone cheese. Cook until the cheese is melted on top of the chicken. Remove from the pan and serve immediately along with angel hair pasta with marinara sauce.

Serves 6

Note: Veal can be substituted for the chicken!

Buon Appetito!

Gnocchi di ricotta

(Ricotta Dumplings)

1 lb ricotta cheese
3 eggs
¾ cup Romano cheese
2 ½ cups all-purpose flour, sifted
1 tbsp butter, melted

Mix all of the ingredients into a large bowl. Knead the mixture until a dough is formed. Cover the bowl and let the dough stand for one hour. Sprinkle some flour on your work board and onto your hands. Take 4 ounces of dough and roll it gently with both hands, forming a long rope about 1 inch thick. Repeat this until all the dough is done. Cut the dough into 1 inch pieces. Set aside and cover with a clean cloth.

Fill a large pot ¾ full with water. Add 2 tablespoons of salt and bring it to a boil. Add the gnocchi to the boiling water. Stir gently. When the gnocchi float to the top, let them cook for an additional 3 minutes. Remove them with a slotted spoon and place them onto a large platter. Scoop some marinara sauce over them and serve immediately.

Serves 6

Buon Appetito!

Involtini di Pesce Spada
(Swordfish Rolls)

8 pieces of swordfish, each piece ¼ inch thick

2 tbsp salt

1 tbsp pepper

16 fresh bay leaves

1 medium onion, chopped

1 cup olive oil

1 cup bread crumbs

1 cup pine nuts

½ cup fresh parsley, chopped

2 tbsp lemon juice

2 tbsp orange juice

½ tsp salt

¼ tsp pepper

1 tbsp sugar

½ cup raisins

Preheat the oven to 400 degrees.

Filling

In a medium skillet, sautée the onion in olive oil until tender. Stir in the bread crumbs and cook until the crumbs are toasted. Remove from heat. Add the pine nuts, parsley, raisins, lemon juice, orange juice, sugar, salt, and pepper, and mix well. Set aside to cool.

Place the fish fillets on a clean, flat counter and sprinkle with salt and pepper. Place a tablespoon of filling in the center of each piece of fish. Roll each piece tightly and secure with a tooth pick. Lightly oil a medium baking pan with olive oil. Place each of the fish rolls onto the pan. Arrange a bay leaf between each roll. Sprinkle olive oil and the remaining filling on top of the fish. Bake for 20 minutes, or until fish are fork tender. Serve immediately.

Serves 8

Buon Appetito!

Pasta con Sarde
(Pasta with Sardines)

1 lb fresh fennel

1½ lbs fresh sardines, cleaned and de-scaled (meat only cut in small pieces)

1½ cups olive oil

1 medium onion, chopped

64 oz tomato sauce (page #)

1 cup pine nuts, toasted

2 cups bread crumbs, toasted, with ½ tsp cinnamon added

2 garlic cloves, chopped

1 lb broccoli florets

1 lb cauliflower, cleaned and cut into small florets

1 cup grated Romano cheese

1 cup flour

½ cup golden raisins

½ tsp cinnamon

1 tsp white pepper

1 tbsp salt

2 tbsp salt

1 lb spaghetti, broken into 2 inch pieces

1 tbsp salt

Fill a large pot with water, and add 2 tablespoons of salt and 1 tablespoon of olive oil. Bring it to a boil. Cook the broccoli and cauliflower until fork tender. Remove them from the pot with a slotted spoon and set them aside. In the same water, cook the fennel until tender, and remove from the pot with a slotted spoon and set aside. Cook the pasta in the same water according to package directions. Once cooked, drain the pasta and keep warm.

Heat ½ cup of olive oil in a large frying pan. Add the onion and garlic, and cook for 1 minute. Add the broccoli, cauliflower, fennel, salt, and pepper. Cook for 5 minutes, stirring often. Remove it from the pan, add pine nuts and raisins, and set it aside. Heat ½ cup of olive oil in a medium frying pan. Coat the sardines with flour, and fry over low heat for about 3 minutes on each side. Drain the sardines on a paper towel, and set them aside. Lay 2 scoops of sauce into a large baking casserole. Add half of the pasta, 2 more scoops of sauce, half of the vegetables, half of the sardines, half of the toasted bread crumbs, and half of the Romano cheese. Mix gently. Repeat the second layer the same as the first. Finish with the remaining sauce poured on top. Sprinkle with Romano cheese. Bake at 400 degrees for 20 minutes.

Serves 6

Buon Appetito!

Sicilian Potato Gnocchi

4 potatoes boiled and mashed
1 ½ cups all purpose flour plus more for dusting
1/2 tsp salt plus 1 tbsp
2 egg yolks, beaten
1 tbsp olive oil
Romano cheese for sprinkling

Flour a baking sheet and set aside.
In a large mixing bowl add potatoes, salt and beaten egg yolks, mix well. Add flour and keep mixing until smooth, about 5 minutes. Take dough out of bowl and place onto a well floured surface. Knead until smooth and elastic, adding more flour if needed. Divide dough into 8 parts. Shape each part into long ropes, making sure to use enough flour to prevent sticking. Cut each rope into one inch pieces. Flour your hands and using your thumb, slightly flatten each piece by pushing down into the dough. Set gnocchi onto floured baking sheet.

Fill a large pot with 8 quarts of water. Add 1 tbsp of salt and 1 tbsp of olive oil and bring to a boil. Cook gnocchi in batches. Boil until they float to the top, then cook for 4 minutes longer. Remove with a slotted spoon and set aside. Keep hot until all gnocchi are cooked. Serve with marinara sauce, sprinkled with Romano cheese.

Serves 8

Buon Appetito!

Pepe Verde Imbottito
(Stuffed Green Peppers)

6 large green peppers
1 small white onion, chopped
8 oz pork sausage
1 lb ground beef
1/4 cup olive oil
4 sprigs fresh parsley, finely chopped
2 large fresh basil leaves, finely chopped
1 garlic clove, minced
1 small pepperoncini, finely chopped
1/8 tsp red pepper flakes
1 tsp salt
1/4 tsp white pepper
3/4 cup Romano cheese, grated
1 ½ cups plain bread crumbs
1 cup of water
2 cups of marinara sauce

Preheat oven to 500 degrees.

Wash green peppers, cut tops off, remove seeds and ribbing from the inside. Set aside.

In a medium skillet heat olive oil over medium heat. Add onions, garlic, parsley and basil and sautee for 3 minutes. Add sausage and ground beef and cook until browned throughout. Add salt, pepper, red pepper flakes and pepperoncinis and cook for one more minute. Remove from heat and set aside.

In a large bowl, combine bread crumbs and Romano cheese, mix well. Add the meat mixture to bowl and mix again, making sure all ingredients are combined well. Using a teaspoon, begin stuffing the green peppers. When all peppers are stuffed, place into a 9x11 baking pan, stuffed end up. Add the cup of water to the bottom of the pan. Cover with aluminum foil and bake at 500 degrees for 30 to 40 minutes.
When peppers are done remove from pan. Plate peppers and pour marinara sauce over them. Serve with your favorite pasta and marinara sauce.

Serves 6

Buon Appetito!

Involtini di Melenzane
(Rolled and stuffed eggplant)

1 large eggplant, cut into 12 slices lengthwise

1 small white onion, finely chopped

1 garlic clove, minced

1 tomato, seeded and chopped

24 fresh spinach leaves

12 slices good Genoa salami

4 oz ricotta cheese

1/8 tsp salt

1/8 tsp white pepper

2 tbsp Romano cheese, grated

1½ cups shredded mozzarella cheese

2 cups marinara sauce

1½ cups olive oil plus 2 tbsps

Preheat oven to 475 degrees.

In a small bowl mix ricotta cheese, Romano cheese and salt and pepper. Set aside. In a large frying pan, heat olive oil over medium heat. Fry each slice of eggplant on both sides until golden brown. Remove and drain on paper towels. Do not layer eggplant on top of each other while draining or slices will stick together. Set aside.

In a small frying pan heat remaining olive oil. Add onions, garlic and sautee for 2 minutes. Add tomato and cook for an additional 5 minutes. Remove from heat and set aside.

Spread marinara sauce evenly on the bottom of a 9x11 baking pan. Assemble eggplant rolls by placing one slice of eggplant on a work surface. Center on the eggplant one slice of salami, 2 pieces of spinach, one teaspoon of the tomato and onion mixture and one teaspoon of ricotta mixture. Make sure all the ingredients are in the middle of the eggplant slice. Beginning from the thin end of the eggplant, roll up each slice and gently set into baking dish with the loose end down. Continue until all eggplant slices are rolled and placed into the pan, one next to another. Sprinkle with mozzarella cheese and bake at 475 degrees for 15 minutes or until cheese is melted and lightly browned.

Serves 4

Buon Appetito!

Polpettini di Carne
(Meatballs)

1 lb ground beef
2 large eggs
1/2 cup Romano cheese, grated
3/4 tsp salt
1/2 tsp black pepper
1 small carrot
2 celery stalks
1 small white onion, finely chopped
1 tbsp chopped parsley
4 fresh basil leaves, finely chopped
1/4 tsp dried oregano
1 cup plain bread crumbs
1/4 tsp garlic powder
1/4 cup olive oil
1/2 cup water

Preheat oven to 475 degrees.

In a food processor, place carrots and celery and process for about 10 seconds or until carrots and celery are very finely chopped.

In a small bowl beat eggs, salt and pepper. Set aside.

In a medium bowl mix ground beef, carrot and celery mixture, garlic, parsley, basil and oregano. Add bread crumbs, Romano cheese and using your hands mix well. Add the eggs and continue to mix until all ingredients are combined well. Let mixture rest for 5 minutes.

On a large baking sheet brush olive oil evenly across the bottom. Dip your hands into a little of the olive oil. Take one heaping tablespoon of the meat into your hands and roll into a ball. Place onto the oiled baking sheet. Continue until all meat is rolled into balls. Bake at 475 degrees for 20 minutes. Take out of the oven, turn meatballs over and bake for an additional 15 minutes. Gently remove meatballs with a spatula and serve along with your favorite pasta or as desired. Any leftover meatballs can be stored in the refrigerator for 5 days.

Yields approximately 25 meatballs.

Buon Appetito!

Printed in the United States
by Baker & Taylor Publisher Services